THE ART &
SCIENCE OF

Assessing General Education Outcomes

A PRACTICAL GUIDE

BY ANDREA LESKES AND BARBARA D. WRIGHT

Association
of American
Colleges and
Universities

1818 R Street, NW, Washington, DC 20009-1604

ISBN 0-9763576-2-3

To order additional copies of this publication or to find out more about other AAC&U

publications, visit www.aacu.org, e-mail pub_desk@aacu.org, or call 202.387.3760.

This publication was made possible by a grant from Carnegie Corporation of New York. The

statements made and views expressed are solely the responsibility of the authors.

Contents

Acknowledgments

*T*HIS MONOGRAPH DRAWS ON THE WORK of many colleges and universities around the country. It also reflects new priorities of regional and specialized accrediting associations that since 1988 have helped focus the higher education community's attention on assessment of student learning. Because of faculty efforts to improve both general education and undergraduate education more broadly, assessment has become a key to institutional renewal. We would particularly like to thank all of the campuses that have sent teams to AAC&U's annual general education institute over the past five years, both while it took place in Asheville, North Carolina, and more recently in Newport, Rhode Island; the serious efforts of team members to review and reform general education programs enriched our understanding of campus endeavors. Colleagues on the institute teaching staff also deserve acknowledgment.

Our approach to assessing general education outcomes is framed by the vision of *Greater Expectations*; all the individuals who participated in that initiative deserve recognition, as do the funders: the Pew Charitable Trusts, Carnegie Corporation of New York, and Fund for the Improvement for Postsecondary Education.

A number of colleagues at AAC&U helped with the publication: Ross Miller through his assessment expertise and database of examples, Gretchen Sauvey by carefully checking for consistency, and Michael Ferguson by copyediting.

Particular thanks are due to Daniel Fallon and Carnegie Corporation of New York for their financial support and patience.

The Contemporary Context

THE REPORT *GREATER EXPECTATIONS: A NEW VISION FOR LEARNING AS A NATION GOES TO COLLEGE*, released by the Association of American Colleges and Universities (AAC&U) in 2002, presents an inspiring, contemporary view of liberal learning. The *Greater Expectations* vision is challenging enough in itself but becomes even more so when we ask how American colleges and universities will assess such learning. This guide is designed to supply practical assistance as faculties assess some of the most complex and important outcomes of college study. It offers an introduction to the assessment process, a series of logical steps campuses can follow to answer their key questions about student learning, and some commonsense advice for maintaining the momentum and usefulness of the assessment process. The current concern with general education and its assessment forms the context for this pragmatic advice and leads naturally to a discussion of the public interest in liberal learning. The final chapter and the appendix provide tools for the academic practitioner.

The term "general education" carries varied meanings: core texts, required courses, a common curriculum, a distribution requirement. For the purposes of this publication, general education will be interpreted more expansively to mean the part of an undergraduate or liberal education curriculum that is shared by all students, a definition drawn from *Greater Expectations*. Such a definition allows general education to take many shapes while it continues to introduce multiple disciplines and to form the foundation for crucial intellectual and civic capacities.

Greater Expectations argues for viewing general education as much more than required courses to be "gotten out of the way" as quickly as possible, to use the current, unfortunate parlance. Rather, it should serve as the keystone of an integrated and coherent arch of liberal learning. "General learning" is certainly expected to occur in structured general education programs, because it provides a foundation for students' subsequent disciplinary study and for success in their areas of concentration. However, such learning is too vital to be compartmentalized; it also needs to be pursued in an intentional manner elsewhere in an undergraduate education. No one part of the curriculum (or even, one might add, the entire formal curriculum alone) can be solely responsible for developing such important and complex abilities as critical thinking, information literacy, intercultural communication, or teamwork skills; these capacities require reinforcement from all curricular and educational elements over an extended period of time. The major field serves as the locus for students' most advanced college study and, as such, provides the content and the context in which they can develop knowledge and intellectual skills at a sophisticated level before graduation. Work over the past decade, much of it published by AAC&U, has emphasized the need for general education and the major to support one another in creating a strong, coherent program of learning.

Assessing general education poses a particular challenge because often it has lofty but ill-defined goals, a diffuse structure, and minimal faculty oversight. Given the central importance of general education in the arch of liberal learning, however, it is essential that institutions rise to the challenge. In addition to improving actual learning, the assessment process can potentially, if indirectly, address other problems perennially associated with general education: low status, departmental neglect, curricular fragmentation, and surface learning. A campus-wide embrace of assessment can promote better understanding of the purposes of general education and remedy its neglect on the part of students and faculty alike.

This is an ideal time to publish a guide on assessing general education outcomes because five strands of work on improving undergraduate education are converging in an effort to assure quality and accountability at the very heart of college-level learning.

1. Continuing attention to general education review and reform. A national survey (Ratcliff et al. 2001) confirmed that general education was a high priority for academic leaders and faculty (on 57 percent of responding campuses, a formal review of the general education program was underway). Not only is general education undergoing examination and revision for its own sake; given its place at the center of undergraduate study, it also drives undergraduate curricular reform and institutional change more broadly.

2. Growing interest in assessment. Only a decade ago, academics tended to view assessment as externally imposed, a threat to faculty autonomy, and irrelevant to the "real work" of college study. This situation is starting to change, however, as campus practitioners come to understand assessment as an essential tool for educational improvement rather than simply a way to meet external demands for accountability. Today, conferences and workshops on assessment draw record audiences, assessment publications fly off the shelves, and assessment consultants find themselves in great demand.

OFTEN CONFUSED TERMS

"Liberal education" should not be understood narrowly, as describing either specific subject matter or a particular type of college. Rather it refers to an approach to learning in which students grapple with complex issues and develop the ability to think for themselves and question their beliefs.

Liberal education: A philosophy of education that empowers individuals, liberates the mind from ignorance, and cultivates social responsibility. Characterized by challenging encounters with important issues, and more a way of studying than specific content, liberal education can occur at all types of colleges and universities. "General education" (see below) and an expectation of in-depth study in at least one field normally comprise liberal education.

Liberal arts: Specific disciplines (the humanities, social sciences, and sciences).

Liberal arts colleges: A particular institutional type— often small, often residential— that facilitates close interaction between faculty members and students, while grounding its curriculum in the liberal arts disciplines.

General education: The part of a liberal education curriculum shared by all students. It provides broad exposure to multiple disciplines and forms the basis for developing important intellectual and civic capacities. General education can take many different forms.

Adapted from *Greater Expectations: A New Vision for Learning as a Nation Goes to College* (AAC&U 2002, 25).

3. Accreditation's enhanced emphasis on student learning as the key indicator of institutional effectiveness. Accreditation agencies have significantly raised their expectations for assessment of student learning, a change that, in turn, has contributed directly to growing campus interest. The standards of both regional (institutional) and specialized (program) accreditors now go beyond simply requiring a process for assessment to be in place. They stress outcomes, demonstrated achievement of student learning, and use of the assessment results in a cycle of improvement. The presence of a well-functioning system of assessment has become the cornerstone of program or institutional effectiveness.

4. **Greater Expectations** *as a framing vision for contemporary, high-quality undergraduate education.* AAC&U's *Greater Expectations* report (2002), which has influenced conversations and action at colleges and universities around the country, contains direct implications for the assessment of general education outcomes. *Greater Expectations* emphasizes the need for clarity about the desired liberal learning outcomes of college; it stresses intentional institutional practices—including assessment as part of a culture of evidence—to achieve these outcomes; and it provides concrete suggestions for directly assessing student work.

5. The publication of **Our Students' Best Work: A Framework for Accountability Worthy of Our Mission** (2004a). This AAC&U statement tackles the thorny issue of higher education's need to demonstrate accountability to external audiences. It proposes a focus on five key educational outcome areas, all fundamental to general education, that are widely affirmed as critically important in undergraduate study: analytic, quantitative, and communication skills; facility with modes of inquiry; intercultural knowledge and collaboration skills; a sense of social and personal responsibility; and the ability to transfer learning from one context to another. *Our Students' Best Work* further advocates milestone assessments *in context* to both promote and demonstrate high-level learning. Aggregation of the results from individual students or courses can then be used to satisfy external demands, while the evidence collected remains anchored in higher education's values, central work, and most promising practices. Only in this way, and not through the use of generic, standardized tests administered at a single point in time, can the public be assured of higher education's success in producing students well prepared for life in the twenty-first century. ■

An Introduction to the Assessment Process

ARE STUDENTS LEARNING WHAT THE FACULTY EXPECTS THEM TO LEARN? How well are they doing so? How can this learning be demonstrated? How might it be improved?

These are the basic questions of assessment—difficult questions about the core learning of general education that no institution can ignore. The *Greater Expectations* vision, while acknowledging the centrality of general education, suggests that a liberal education for the contemporary world encompasses much more than specific general education courses. It involves nourishing the skills, knowledge, and dispositions needed by all students (both for individual success and for responsible citizenship) and by society (for the demands of the workplace and of a globally interconnected world). These capacities should develop throughout the college years: in a student's major, minor, elective courses, extracurricular activities, and in community settings.

This bold vision requires an equally ambitious understanding of assessment. Assessment can serve three important functions: it can inform students about their performance; demonstrate that an institution is fulfilling its mission; and most importantly, provide information for continuous improvement of student learning and program effectiveness. To accomplish these ends, however, higher education cannot confine itself, in the words of *Greater Expectations*, to "limited interpretations of assessment" (AAC&U 2002, 40).

Whether focused on individual students, on courses, on programs, or on the institution as a whole, assessment is the key tool for understanding (1) how well a program of learning works, and (2) how to make it better. The literature contains many definitions of assessment, but a particularly robust one describes assessment as a process of inquiry and improvement. This systematic process consists of

- setting goals and framing questions about student learning;
- gathering evidence to demonstrate how well the goals are achieved;
- interpreting the evidence and designing a plan to improve;
- implementing changes for better learning.

Then the cycle begins anew, perhaps to examine whether the changes introduced in curricular design or teaching practices have produced the desired effect, or perhaps to assess another learning goal. The ultimate aim of assessment is to enhance the positive effect of college practices on student learning and development.

While more elaborate definitions include, for example, planning, mapping, reporting, or assessing-the-assessment steps, all versions follow this basic outline (see, for example, Maki 2002; Palomba and Banta 1999; Rogers 2004; Angelo 1995). The graphic representation of this cycle—the assessment loop—although usually applied to curricular outcomes, can readily be adapted to cocurricular or extracurricular areas and also to student services.

Traditionally, academics excel at defining the *inputs* of a college education. Particularly in the area of general education, untold hours of faculty discussion have gone into debating the content and architecture of programs (the kinds and required number of courses) and rationalizing the final choices. The underlying assumption has been that if one could only identify the ideal inputs, then the desired student learning would naturally follow. If by chance reality fell short of the ideal, the fault would lie with the students who were not smart or industrious enough. Yet all instructors know that good teaching does not necessarily equate to good learning. Assessment challenges the academy to abandon such assumptions and instead define educational success in terms of demonstrated outcomes of the learning process. By changing the focus of institutional attention, a new paradigm emerges, shifting efforts from teaching to learning, from teacher-centered to student-centered education (Barr and Tagg 1995; Tagg 2003).

The last twenty years have witnessed an evolution in the understanding of assessment, with today's practices stressing local approaches, relying increasingly on qualitative methods, and examining as indicators of achievement actual student work products rather than surrogates (e.g., self-reports). Faculty members have become collaborators in creating assessment methods rather than simply bystanders to externally imposed testing regimes. Today in the academy one sees a growing awareness that assessment's primary purpose is to improve learning, with accountability best served through a commitment to continuous improvement.

One of the most powerful uses of assessment arises from teaching students to be self-assessors who can skillfully apply to their own work criteria and analytical procedures similar to those of an expert. The imperative to share assessment methods and results both with students and with colleagues has replaced the notion of assessment as fixed and secret. Through these education-friendly developments, assessment has become a more engaging and powerful aspect of the teaching-learning process. However, confusion continues on campuses about the assumptions, methods, purposes, and even the basic vocabulary of assessment. A campus will do well to begin its assessment initiatives by creating a set of common understandings. The assessment glossary from *Peer Review*'s special issue on value-added assessment is a useful starting point (Leskes 2002). ■

CHAPTER 3

Assessment, Step-by-Step

*H*OW CAN A CAMPUS DESIGN SYSTEMATIC ASSESSMENTS that function as an integrated process of inquiry to improve general education learning outcomes? This section of the guide outlines six steps that a college or university's faculty can follow. The appendix includes a summary of the steps, as a checklist that can be duplicated.

> *"Science does*
> *not know*
> *its debt to*
> *imagination."*
> Ralph Waldo Emerson

Step 1: Understand the mission, values, traditions, and aspirations of your institution and the role of general education in advancing them.

Situated at the center of undergraduate study, general education reflects an institution's identity as does no other part of the curriculum. In reviewing or reforming general education, the faculty needs to consider the campus's guiding mission, intellectual and religious or cultural traditions, educational vision, student population, and aspirations. Most importantly, the faculty must understand how its broad learning goals for students flow from all these factors.

Assessment is not an end in itself but merely a tool for ensuring that programs reflect an institution's aspirations and that students achieve the desired learning. What the tool is used for influences both what is assessed and how such assessment proceeds. Clarity about institutional values can help ensure that assessment serves a vital function by improving what is most important, rather than becoming a trivial, disconnected "exercise in measuring what's easy" (Astin et al. 1992, 2). In concrete terms this means, for example, that if a college prides itself on teamwork, it should design assessment efforts to reflect this value; a church-affiliated institution with a history of spiritual self-reflection would want to build that tradition into its approach to assessment.

Questions to consider:

- What are our institution's values, intellectual traditions, or guiding principles that should be evident in the general education program?
- What distinguishes education at our institution?
- What makes our general education distinctive from that at comparable campuses?
- How are our intellectual traditions or values reflected in our approach to assessment? Is there congruence between educational ends and assessment means?

Step 2: Define key learning goals for your students.

The assessment loop begins with the articulation of learning goals. It is crucial that the goals include what is important to the institution, not merely what seems easy to measure. These goals should apply across the entire spectrum of liberal learning and include content knowledge, of course, but also skills, dispositions, and values. Excluding important goals because they are difficult to measure risks marginalizing them, and yet many of the most valued outcomes of college education fall into this category. Goals may be defined in a very general manner at this point in the process; greater specificity will follow in the next step. However, even early on, the goals should represent faculty agreement on the central shared educational aims for all undergraduates, regardless of their areas of concentration.

Traditionally, the learning that results from college education has received much less attention than inputs (distribution schemes, required courses, numbers of credit hours, etc.). Starting in the late twentieth century, however, national debates about educational quality began to change that balance, and *Greater Expectations* has moved the conversation forward significantly by offering a substantive set of possible outcomes. Students who complete an engaged and practical contemporary liberal education, the report suggests, will be able to adapt to the rapidly changing demands of the labor market while also playing responsible roles in civil society and leading satisfying personal lives. To accomplish all this, they will need a breadth of knowledge and experience, intellectual skills, mental flexibility, and strong ethical grounding. Such "intentional learners"

- can integrate learning and apply it to new situations;
- are empowered through intellectual and practical skills;
- are informed by deep and broad knowledge from many fields;
- are responsible for their own values and the values of the larger society.

Recent work has revealed a growing consensus on the important goals of an undergraduate education among those responsible for higher education quality control at the institutional and the professional programmatic levels (AAC&U 2004b). Both regional and specialized accrediting associations agree that the learning traditionally associated with a liberal education is also the best preparation for the twenty-first-century workplace. Even beyond the accreditation community, business leaders acknowledge, as do faculty members across the country, that a powerful contemporary education will develop communication skills, critical thinking, the ability to integrate knowledge, skill in interpersonal relationships, comfort with diversity and multiple viewpoints, an ethical perspective, content knowledge, and commitment to lifelong learning.

INTENTIONAL LEARNERS

Intentional learners are prepared to thrive in a complex, interdependent, diverse, and constantly changing world. Ready to adapt to new environments and integrate knowledge from various sources, they will continue learning throughout their lives.

SUCH LEARNERS ARE
EMPOWERED through

- communication skills
- analytical and problem-solving skills
- information literacy
- strong powers of observation, judgment, and action
- intellectual agility
- creativity
- teamwork and consensus-building skills

INFORMED through

- broad and deep knowledge from many fields
- familiarity with various modes of inquiry
- experience with the human imagination and its artifacts
- understanding of the world's cultures
- knowledge of science and technology
- familiarity with the histories underlying U.S. democracy

RESPONSIBLE for their personal and civic values through

- intellectual honesty
- ethical action
- a commitment to social justice
- an understanding of self and respect for others
- active participation in civic life

Adapted from *Greater Expectations* (AAC&U 2002, 21–24).

At the same time, such goals for "general learning" should reflect the institution's particular mission, values, traditions, and student needs (referred to in step 1). Following are a few examples of how institutions have individualized student learning goals:

- At Otterbein College, general education stresses the overarching goal of understanding human nature.

- The centrality of internationalism at the American University of Paris finds its way into a statement of learning goals that speaks of skills in encoding, decoding, and translating (ideas, words, images, information, mathematical principles), and also of the multicultural world's primacy as a context for learning.

- Trinity University in Washington, DC, is dedicated to educating women for leadership, community service, and the search for meaning.

Each of these institutions has developed general education architecture to intentionally advance the desired goals. They have recognized that aspirations like these should extend beyond catalog copy to become an integral element in the assessment of general education.

Questions to consider:

- What does the faculty agree that all students graduating from our institution should know and be able to do?

- What skills, capacities, and knowledge will prepare our students—whatever their areas of concentration—for the complex, diverse, and globally interdependent world of the twenty-first century?

- Are these goals widely known and owned by the entire campus community? How can we enhance buy-in?

Step 3: Turn your broad learning goals into assessable outcomes; specify the level of accomplishment desired.

Once broad learning goals are agreed upon, they must be made more specific and ultimately expressed as action verbs to guide curricular design, the choice of classroom practices, and assessment. For example, to say "students will be expected to understand the scientific method" begs the question of what a student can do who has such understanding. A more precise description might include the abilities to formulate hypotheses, gather evidence, draw conclusions, and reason deductively, as illustrated in the following venerable but still excellent example:

UNDERSTANDING THE SCIENTIFIC METHOD: OBJECTIVES IN SCIENCE

I. Ability to recognize and state problems:
The student is expected to
- recognize and identify the central problem
- indicate whether nonscientific factors (e.g., value judgments) are contained in the problem

II. Ability to select, analyze, and evaluate information in relation to a problem:
The student is expected to
- recognize when given information is inadequate
- evaluate the authenticity of given sources of information
- apply information to a given problem's solution

III. Ability to recognize, state, and test hypotheses and other tentative explanations:
The student is expected to
- formulate or recognize hypotheses based on given data
- identify the evidence necessary to judge the truth of a given deduction
- formulate an experiment to test a hypothesis
- recognize when data support the hypothesis, and to what degree

IV. Ability to formulate, recognize, and evaluate conclusions:
The student is expected to
- recognize generalization(s) in a conclusion
- detect unstated assumptions
- recognize when evidence is adequate for a conclusion
- distinguish between deduction and induction
- differentiate between fact and assumption

V. Ability to recognize and formulate attitudes and take action after critical consideration:
The student is expected to
- recognize proper or improper use of such concepts as causality and the tentative nature of truth
- assess a situation and recognize appropriate action in harmony with the nature of science and society

Adapted from Dressel and Mayhew 1954.

As Dressel and Mayhew's work demonstrates, goals need to be divided into hierarchical levels of specificity. While the overarching learning goal ("Understanding the Scientific Method") and its subsections ("Ability to . . .") remain constant, performance indicators can allow for variation and adaptation to different settings. In a similar manner, the various facets of all broad learning goals would need to be teased out, articulated as clear outcomes, and translated into performance measures.

But goals need to be conceived in three dimensions. It is not simply a question of "*What* are we looking for?" but "How *well* is it demonstrated?" and "What happens *over time?*" The more explicitly outcomes are defined, the better they lend themselves to assessment. The more clearly a faculty can describe levels of accomplishment and express expectations for learning at the beginning, middle, and end of a program of study, the better students and the faculty members themselves can respond.

SPECIFIC OUTCOMES AND OBJECTIVES

At **King's College (PA)**, one of the broad learning goals (called "Transferable Skills of Liberal Learning") is effective writing. Each department rearticulates the skill in terms of learning outcomes for its majors. For the biology department, effective writing means the ability "to write in a clear, coherent, concise, and forceful manner both laboratory reports and papers on scientific topics." The specific objectives along the way, starting in the freshman core writing course and leading to senior-year specialized biology courses, progress from the elementary skills of organization and revision to the advanced level of writing a "research paper on original scientific work of a quality that is acceptable for publication." Clear assessment criteria accompany each level of competency.

The **Northeastern University** faculty clarified the broad goal of information literacy by explaining how technological skill is necessary but insufficient: students must know how to locate, extract, critically evaluate, and synthesize information from a variety of sources. Their education should help them to use competently tools appropriate to particular fields, as well as to employ information ethically and in the service of society. The definition leaves room for academic departments to further refine the definition and for the faculty to choose appropriate assessment tools.

Such refinement need not be a highly abstract, speculative process. Professors can start with examples of student work that represent a broad range of performance levels, from basic to very high, divide them into rough categories (e.g., minimal, adequate, proficient, and exemplary), and then describe the common qualities of the artifacts in each category. By approaching the task both deductively and inductively, faculty members can triangulate the qualities of the work before them with the goals and proficiency levels they expect, thereby reaching clarity about the characteristics of mediocrity or excellence.

Rubrics are tools that merge the criteria for the goal (the "what") with a rating scale (the "how well"). Rubrics offer consistent sets of descriptors to which student work can be compared by both professors and students themselves. Assessments based on rubrics may certainly involve subjective judgments, but they adhere to consistent standards. The work of developing criteria and rubrics forces faculty members to produce collectively a written description of what might have begun as an intuition or swift holistic judgment. While an individual professor who says "I know it when I see it" may have a very accurate perception of quality, such a subjective reaction lacks the specific detail needed to explain expectations either to students or to faculty colleagues. Consistency across courses and professors is more likely when the concepts are discussed and positions clarified while examining samples of student work. For accountability purposes (whether related to accreditation or state mandates), an institution will need to articulate clearly the complex abilities desired and show why purely descriptive data or the exclusive use of standardized test scores are inadequate indicators of student proficiency. The last chapter of this guide includes examples of rubrics.

Out of the specification of goals and skill levels—producing criteria, rating scales, and rubrics—questions should arise about student learning and development over time. For example, in examining students' ability to communicate, it is completely legitimate to ask: What *kind* of communication? For what purposes? The answers may be: oral and written communication for informational, expressive, and persuasive purposes. If so, the follow-up question then becomes: just how successful are our students at informing, expressing, and persuading through writing and speaking? With this degree of clarity, reviewers are in a better position to evaluate the work more precisely and identify a differentiated set of strengths and weaknesses. Faculty members may discover, for example, that students are quite capable of expressive communication but less competent at informing and persuading. They may further pinpoint as the crux of the difficulty with informational communication an inability to summarize succinctly or logically. Failure to tailor the appeal to a particular audience may be at the heart of unsuccessful persuasion. Additional analyses may reveal that while students progress significantly in their ability to inform in writing using knowledge gained in their course work, they may advance little in choosing culturally appropriate ways to communicate with diverse audiences. Any and all of these findings suggest paths to improvement.

To provide a useful point of departure for the rest of the assessment process, goals and outcomes must lead to compelling, nontrivial questions about learning that the faculty commits to answering. Articulating goals, criteria, and performance expectations (or standards) for beginning, intermediate, and advanced students is an indispensable step. When looking at complex work products or performances, reviewers must know what they are looking *for*, what questions they are trying to answer, so they can make sense of all the student-generated material.

Questions to consider:

- Have our broad learning goals been subdivided into more specific outcomes and performance indicators?
- What exactly do we expect our students to know and be able to do with their knowledge in their freshman, sophomore, junior, and senior years?
- How much, and in what ways, do we want our students' level of achievement to increase from novice to advanced over their years of college study?
- What burning questions does our faculty most want to answer?

Step 4: Select methods for gathering evidence of learning that are appropriate to your desired goals and outcomes.

Once faculty members have clarified the questions they want to answer, they can proceed to the next assessment step, that of making a reasoned choice of method. To continue with the example of written communication, a campus expecting students to develop and demonstrate persuasive argumentation through writing will not make the mistake of administering a multiple-choice test that requires nothing more than identifying spelling, punctuation, or sentence-structure errors. Nor will it rely on a questionnaire that asks students to self-assess whether they learned how to write well.

Aligning assessment methods with learning goals means

- using direct methods to examine student work products;
- choosing those direct methods that can produce evidence of the goal(s) in question at a high level of complexity;
- applying those methods at the most appropriate points in a course or a curriculum.

Direct methods allow faculty members to look at real examples of student work and make judgments about what students know and can do. Such methods include live or recorded performances, capstone projects, research papers, portfolios (traditional and electronic), presentations, essay examinations, and other evidence of learning. While these approaches may appear more cumbersome than traditional short-answer testing, they have significant advantages. Most importantly, they produce rich, accurate, usable information about complex learning outcomes: information that can powerfully improve learning in a local context. But collecting such products of student effort is also efficient and has face validity[1] because the evidence can be generated through assignments already required as part of a course. (See assessment methods in chapter 6.)

The best evidence of learning is *direct* evidence: student work and performances that can be examined to determine what students know and can do. Traditional approaches to assessment often rely on *indirect* evidence (e.g., responses to surveys, self-reports) and descriptive data (e.g., completion rates or time to degree). Such indirect evidence can help identify problem areas and provide useful information (on what students *think* they learned, for example). If an institution's general education has as a goal the ability to integrate knowledge from many sources but students report on surveys that they had few opportunities to practice this skill, the campus would want to review the curricular structure. However, indirect methods cannot answer fundamental questions about learning. They can neither reveal what successful integration of knowledge from many sources actually looks like in student papers or projects, nor how well students are able to accomplish this task.

Traditional testing does provide direct evidence of what students know and is a widely accepted assessment method. Complex examinations, when well constructed, can probe deep knowledge and intellectual skills. Since such exams are often used within courses to test content knowledge acquired in the course, the results will answer questions related to that knowledge acquisition. Traditional testing is less frequently used to gather evidence about learning that extends beyond the confines of a single course or develops over time, although certainly exams can be designed and administered to do so.

Tests based on standardized true/false and multiple-choice questions, however, generally measure knowledge at a superficial and formula-based level while sending the message to students that successful education equates to swift, decontextualized recall and regurgitation of facts. This is hardly the rich understanding of general education that academics want to encourage or that *Greater Expectations* promotes. Not surprisingly, students can best demonstrate higher-order intellectual skills when given assignments or activities that demand this type of cognition. (For various definitions of higher-order intellectual processes, see Anderson et al. 2001; Bloom 1956; Entwistle 2001; Marra 2002; Perry 1970; Resnick 1987.)

With increasing frequency, institutions are choosing to assess learning by embedding assessment in the normal proceedings of a class and examining the work products generated (such as library research papers, essays, case-study analyses, field research, community-service projects, or performances). These tasks are considered authentic because they mimic the situations or problem solving that students might experience in real-world settings. Beyond their face validity and relevance to the learning experience, these assessment approaches ask students to demonstrate an integrated mastery of

HIGHER-ORDER THINKING

- is non-algorithmic (the path of action is not fully specified in advance)
- is complex (the totality is not visible from any single vantage point)
- often yields multiple solutions
- requires nuanced judgment and interpretation
- involves application of multiple, possibly conflicting criteria
- often involves uncertainty (not everything is or can be known)
- requires self-regulation (no one else gives directions)
- involves making meaning (discerning patterns in apparent disorder)
- requires effort and time

Adapted from Resnick 1987.

---

[1] Face validity: seems to be a reasonable way to proceed; on "the face of it" provides valid information about the outcome of interest.

complex knowledge, skills, and dispositions, and to do so in open-ended, unscripted ways. They require judgment in the face of conflicting evidence or multiple solutions, with students actively constructing their own responses verbally, graphically, mathematically, or representationally. The richness of such assessment methods contrasts starkly with the more limited demands of traditional short-answer testing.

The development of embedded methods has facilitated assessment of elusive but crucial learning goals that would be eliminated if faculty members were to restrict themselves to readily measurable goals. Acknowledging that what is gained in validity may be lost in reliability[2] (although this loss can be mitigated by the aforementioned faculty conversations on standards), assessment practitioners are embracing qualitative, descriptive approaches along with quantitative ones and accepting that assessment ultimately is as much judgment as statistics, as much art as science.

By aligning assessment methods with outcomes one can increase the possibility of collecting information that answers significant questions or leads to improvement. Too often, however, instead of allowing key educational questions to drive the choice of instrument or method, off-the-shelf instruments have been allowed to shape assessment questions. Early attention to the goals, criteria, and rubrics that influence the selection of methods will help ensure the collection of direct, relevant, useful evidence of student learning.

Beyond being aligned with goals, methods need to be owned by the campus. Faculty buy-in happens more frequently when the approach has been developed in-house or adapted to local circumstances. Finally, methods need to have consequential validity. In other words, they should lead to the desired results: rich evidence of learning or programmatic strengths and weaknesses; productive conversations across traditional boundaries; actions for improvement; and substance for communication with external audiences.

Questions to consider:
- What assessment method or methods would best provide direct evidence of learning to answer our questions?
- What are we already doing that can also serve assessment purposes?
- What methods would be in keeping with our mission and values?

[2] Validity: reflects the learning it is designed to measure. Reliability: provides consistent results over time given constant conditions.

Step 5: Determine the crucial points at which you need to gather evidence.

The best assessment can be described not as a snapshot but as a movie. Rather than merely offering a cross-sectional picture of students' knowledge or skills at one particular moment, it provides a developmental view over time and across individual courses. Such a longitudinal representation can show what students have achieved in absolute terms as well as their growth since beginning college and the remaining distance to travel. Creating a developmental record of growth and progress—whether of an individual student, a cohort of students, a program, or an entire institution—requires effort but promises potentially powerful insights and guidance for improvement. Unlike a snapshot, a movie can reveal not only progress but also plateaus or even regression. General education in the spirit of *Greater Expectations* must foster sophisticated knowledge and skills continuously, across the entire span of the undergraduate education. Assessment needs to trace that arc as well.

While campuses can gather evidence at many points during the undergraduate years to construct a picture of student learning over time, comprehensive assessment is still uncommon. The problem is not lack of opportunity but rather a failure to design assessment coherently and inclusively. Writing, for example, is often assessed at the end of a first-year, two-semester composition sequence, but anything beyond that point tends to be erratic or serendipitous. If subsequent written communication assessment does occur in a "W-designated" course or in the major, it is usually without input from faculty members who taught students writing two or three years earlier.

In collecting documentation to yield a moving picture of student learning, one will want to look at knowledge and foundational skills, but also at the acquisition of inquiry strategies, at collaborative and practical skills, and at examined values. Ideally evidence would come from the beginning of the college experience (first-year programs and introductory courses), the middle (as students select majors and minors and begin to take intermediate level electives), and finally the senior year. By then, one would be looking for advanced learning, at a sophisticated level, often applied within the context of the major. Work products might come from culminating performances, capstone projects, research, professional practicum placements, internships, student government leadership, or community service.

In particular, a campus would want to examine how the major deepens the intellectual skills and knowledge of general education. Advanced study in the major, for example, can provide the complex content which students would be expected to communicate to multiple audiences, evaluate for ethical implications, and connect with other disciplines. *Taking Responsibility for the Quality of the Baccalaureate Degree* (AAC&U 2004b) describes some excellent senior capstones that build on prior preparation in the curriculum and ask students to apply multiple aspects of their knowledge in new ways.

As interest in assessment evolves, novice practitioners may find themselves confused by the terms "formative" and "summative." Formative assessment is most usefully understood to mean that it occurs "along the way," providing feedback to improve the learning of individual students (or programs) as they progress toward a goal. Summative assessment, in contrast, asks endpoint questions: What does this course or educational experience add up to? What has the student achieved? Does this meet campus aspirations for any individual student? For students collectively? Summative assessment can improve the learning of the next cohort of students.

At first glance, it may seem as if endpoint questions arise most appropriately when students graduate, and, indeed, the senior year is a logical time for summative assessments. But many other points exist at which to take stock of progress, and knowing about student accomplishments at these moments can inform curricular or pedagogical choices. The conclusion of a first-year experience, the completion of lower-division prerequisites for the major, or the last general education requirement are several such touch points. In fact, most of these points are both an end and a beginning, just as graduation is also called commencement: the start of a new phase of life and of new learning that builds on the phase just concluded.

Similarly, most assessments can have both formative and summative value, depending upon the emphasis and use of the evidence. As a result, distinguishing between assessment and evaluation by identifying the former as formative and the latter as summative is not terribly useful. Done properly, *all* assessment serves improvement by answering questions that may be formative, summative, or both. However, assessment does differ from evaluation in that it neither assigns a grade to any individual nor carries specific rewards or punishments.

An essential element of planning for assessment, then, is to select data-gathering points that allow the documentation of progress over time. A campus's faculty, collectively, must decide

- which are the most important touch points (keeping the number manageable);
- what kinds of evidence will best reflect the overarching goals for liberal learning and general education across many courses and other learning experiences;
- how the information will be used for constructive change.

While comprehensive, the plan needs to be lean and sustainable, focusing on essential outcomes and the efficient collection of evidence to assess several outcomes at the same time. A senior thesis, for example, could be used to assess simultaneously critical thinking, written communication, quantitative literacy, and in-depth knowledge. The assessment planning matrix in the appendix can serve as a guide for campuses developing such comprehensive assessment plans.

Questions to consider:

- What exactly are our expectations for students' development of knowledge, skills, and values over time?
- What are students already doing, in class or beyond, that can generate evidence for assessment purposes?
- Which are the most important data-collection points in our curriculum and for which outcomes?
- Are our plans effective yet manageable? How will we use the evidence gathered?

Step 6: Close the improvement loop by ensuring that you interpret and use the evidence collected.

Too often, assessment is viewed as a matter of administering an instrument and reporting the results to satisfy external accountability demands. This limited notion is foreign both to the *Greater Expectations* vision and to the need for better student achievement. However, even attempts to use assessment for improved learning may fail to close the assessment loop if the final steps go no further than simply sharing the raw data. Such an abbreviated process incorrectly assumes that people will automatically respond and make improvements if presented with evidence. Good assessment practice, on the other hand, calls for tracing the entire assessment loop in a conscious and purposeful manner. Only through thoughtful interpretation and use of evidence does the investment in time and resources pay off in concrete results.

The issue of who will be responsible for interpreting the data—and ultimately converting it into a robust understanding of students' learning—should be resolved early in the process. By drawing on a range of people with varied expertise and perspectives, a campus can ensure a multifaceted interpretive conversation about what the evidence reveals. Such collective analysis is particularly important when assessing general education. Certainly professors who teach general education courses are central to the assessment process but, in fact, all educators have a stake in general learning outcomes—even those who teach very specialized courses. As appropriate, a campus could also include students, librarians, instructors of remedial mathematics or writing, internship supervisors, local employers, student affairs personnel, and faculty from neighboring institutions. This important interpretive step is clearly not simply a job to be assigned to an institutional research office, although such experts in educational data analysis could bring important knowledge to the conversations. By constructing a community of interpretation, a campus can extract meaning on multiple levels, weigh various responses, and then follow up with specific actions. Multiple perspectives can shed light on environmental factors that help or hinder learning while also preventing an excessive focus on disciplines and specialized knowledge.

The benefits of a rich community of interpretation extend beyond the immediate task at hand. Changes in programs and teaching methods will require a broad commitment to continuous improvement; implementation will depend on a network of individuals willing to tackle such practical matters as planning, budgeting, scheduling, faculty development, technology, and governance. In the long term, only the will of the community as a whole can change campus culture.

Questions to consider:

- What are our plans for interpreting evidence? Who will be involved? How will we manage and support the process?

- Are we satisfied with the learning achieved? If not, what changes are needed?

- What resources are required and available to implement proposed changes?

- What obstacles to change exist and how can they be overcome?

- When will we revisit these changes to see whether they were successful?

- How will we communicate and celebrate our successes? ■

Ten Tips for Better Assessment

THE PREVIOUS CHAPTER, WITH ITS SIX STEPS AND RELATED QUESTIONS, can guide a campus toward a comprehensive system of assessment for general education outcomes. Experience has shown, however, that certain advice applies at all stages. The following tips for better assessment (summarized in the appendix on a single page that can be photocopied) serve as down-to-earth reminders for all members of the campus community.

1. Look for evidence of learning, not just statistics.

Worry about *doing* good, not looking good. Keep the focus of assessment on learning, not on surrogates of quality such as incoming SAT scores, the presence of certain types of programs, retention rates, or student satisfaction surveys. For general education, surrogates often include whether a campus offers a first-year program, writing across the curriculum, undergraduate research, service-learning programs, study abroad, etc. A learning environment that includes such options has a high potential to enhance learning, but there is no guarantee that it will, nor does an inventory of these inputs document student achievement.

If external bodies request surrogate statistics for accountability purposes, institutions can provide the data requested and then take the opportunity to explain the meaningful assessments that are occurring on campus to improve learning.

2. Remain focused first on *improving* the quality of student learning, then on assuring its quality.

The debate has persisted for two decades: is assessment undertaken to improve student learning (for internal educational purposes) or to satisfy external demands for accountability? The answer has to be, "for both," but emphasis matters. While assessment for quality improvement can *also* serve quality assurance, an overriding focus on the latter is unlikely to guide internal audiences toward the former.

The concept of assessment encounters least resistance, makes the most sense to faculty members, and provides the greatest benefit to institutions when it is pursued primarily for the purpose of improving the quality of student learning, not merely to certify that learning has occurred. If improved education is the aim, then the most salient comparison for an institution or its general education program is against its own past record. Benchmarking against other campuses or similar programs may be informative but is of secondary interest.

3. Build on what is already occurring.

Most campuses, whether or not they have systematic programs of assessment in place, need not start assessment from scratch. An inventory is likely to reveal many individuals who are already examining student work, collecting data, overseeing portfolios, or gaining insights that then serve to improve various aspects of the educational experience. They may, however, be working in isolation or never have considered how their efforts can serve assessment purposes. They may not have adequate support, understand the assessment cycle, or be part of a community endeavor. Guided by the concept of intentional practice (which essentially means aligning aims and actions), these efforts can become successful—even model—assessment practices; they can serve as corner-stones for coherent assessment programs. Knowing that experiments and models already function on campus can reassure even those who consider themselves novices at formal assessment.

Similarly, in every program on campus, students produce documents and performances that can provide evidence to answer assessment questions. Instead of seeing assessment as an add-on requiring new effort, faculty members can use assignments they already require or make slight adjustments to bring them into alignment with specific general education outcomes and assessment plans. For example, classroom work can be given a "second reading"—this time not to assign an individual grade but to answer an assessment question about, for example, information literacy or critical thinking. A new assessment effort can also build on local talent. Most campuses employ faculty members and administrators with significant assessment-related expertise. Whether in professional programs (particularly education), the performing or visual arts, or institutional research, they know how to write learning outcomes, evaluate portfolios, create authentic assignments, apply rubrics, or construct surveys. The campus that makes good use of this talent can save time and money while also providing recognition to people who may have toiled alone for years.

4. Make assessment ongoing, not episodic.

The greatest benefits from assessment appear when the process is iterative and the effects (whether on curriculum, pedagogy, students, or faculty) cumulative. The concept of "ongoing" may refer to assessment of one outcome over several semesters or to the study of one cohort of students over time. It may mean multiple use of the same sample or the same method. Yet too often assessment is regarded as a matter of gathering some data (which may be more or less related to an actual learning goal), writing a report, and then forgetting about the entire exercise until the next request years later.

Besides contributing to the improvement of cumulative learning, a continuous process helps a campus develop habits of reflection and inquiry about learning. Repeated conversations gradually break down campus silos and provide occasions for students, professors, professional staff, and administrators to participate. A continuous process facilitates the sharing of information and expertise, thereby building collegiality, collaboration, and a collective responsibility for both general education and learning. Ultimately, ongoing assessment can change campus culture, tempering the individuality so treasured by the academy with a sense of common purpose. For faculty and institutions, ongoing assessment may be a fractal image of the lifelong learning they expect students to manifest.

5. Divide the labor, share the responsibility.

No student is the product of a single faculty member, a single course, or a single program. Given contemporary attendance patterns, few students are even the product of a single institution. Moreover, as *Greater Expectations* argues, higher-order intellectual development is cumulative; it happens only over time. The logical conclusion is that assessment cannot be the responsibility of a single faculty member or program, either. In the real academic world, however, professors, departments, and programs also have other work to do, so the task of assessing general education outcomes may be delegated to a committee. The basic principle is to aim for collective responsibility but a division of labor, with the committee communicating frequently, enlisting help as needed (e.g., when an embedded assignment occurs across a range of courses), and sharing its findings on a regular schedule. The faculty as a whole keeps apprised, supports the process, and cooperates in implementing recommended changes.

6. Do not let the perfect be the enemy of the good.

Most campuses will not arrive at the definitive list of general education outcomes, will not develop ideal rubrics or have flawless teaching, a fully coherent curriculum, absolute consensus, or 100 percent student achievement at the highest level. In the pursuit of perfection madness lies, but fortunately perfection is not required. The questions are rather: What constitutes high quality in our graduates? What degree of success is acceptable? How can we increase the proportion of students who reach these acceptable levels? How can assessment help us continuously improve? And how can we continuously improve our assessments? To avoid paralysis, a campus is well advised to remember that assessment is an ongoing, flexible, naturally evolving process offering many opportunities to fine-tune or change direction. Meanwhile, even an imperfect process can yield useful results.

7. Prioritize.

Wise educators know that in teaching it often makes sense to scale back coverage to ensure deep understanding. In other words, less is more if it leads to learning that lasts. They know, similarly, that in assessment it is impossible to assess every outcome in every course; in fact, trying to do so may well prove counterproductive.

A well-planned assessment effort identifies a list of key learning goals for general education and then develops a sustainable plan for managing assessment. This may mean distributing responsibility (for example, assigning each of several committees a specific outcome), or taking several years to cycle through a list of goals, or using sampling techniques. It will probably mean choosing strategic points for assessment, rather than attempting to monitor a selected goal every semester in every course. An in-depth look at a few goals is more likely to produce useful information than an attempt to assess many in superficial ways. Well-planned assessment means gathering the right amount of useful evidence—no more and no less. Useful in this case means agreed upon, relevant, lending itself to appropriate analysis, and expected to produce concrete improvements.

Remember, if an assessment effort starts with unrealistic plans and then collapses under its own weight, not only does the improvement effort suffer, but commitment to assessment weakens and the political damage can carry long-term consequences.

8. Experiment, take risks, be creative.

Assessment offers an opportunity for a campus and its faculty to be self-reflective, inventive, and pioneering in undergraduate education. It provides common work to anchor conversations about important general education goals, many of which can be quite difficult to validate. Seizing the opportunity to use existing approaches (conventional or unconventional, quantitative or qualitative, or a combination of all) can advance understanding of student learning. Going further and piloting new methods, deeply probing how a general education program transforms student intellectual development over time, gathering authentic evidence in ways that resonate with the institution's values, and contributing to the advancement of the field can reenergize the entire teaching and learning process.

While assessment results may provide positive validation, they may also reveal deficiencies. A campus will do well not to shy away from bad news. The aim of assessment is not to prove but to *improve*. Public acknowledgment of weaknesses models for students how to deal candidly with problems and move on to solutions. Assessment should be applied precisely where its insights can lead to the greatest positive changes.

9. Tell the whole story.

Assessment well done makes a wonderful story. When an institution examines its students' learning of general education outcomes, interprets the evidence, and uses the discoveries in an intentional manner to make changes that improve achievement, it has a right to be proud. Unfortunately, the telling often falls short by describing only the process and data; the concerns that motivated the inquiry, the institution-specific rationale for choices, and the insights gained should also be shared. Relating the whole story, with its successes and failures, trials and tribulations—on campus, to external colleagues, and to other stakeholders—is a way for the entire academy to bear witness to its serious responsibility for student learning. It will also help the public understand the complexity of the learning process and why thoughtful, systematic examination of "our students' best work" is the responsible way to approach improvement and accountability.

10. Remember that assessment is both old and new.

At first glance, assessment may seem foreign and intrusive to faculty, but it is not entirely new or alien. Professors have traditionally discussed cutting-edge discoveries in their disciplines and how they might influence the curriculum and pedagogical choices. Testing and grading have long been used to uphold standards and provide feedback to students and their instructors. These practices have worked well as far as they go.

Assessment builds on these academic traditions but raises them to the next power. For example, assessment uses the format of department or committee meetings, but asks faculty members to supplement individual impressions with evidence and analysis. Unlike grading, assessment is collective rather than private; systematic rather than ad hoc. It asks questions not simply about one course or one student, but also about what the program as a whole adds up to. This question of total impact is of particular importance in a program as sprawling, unsupervised, and yet essential as general education. Good assessment is intentional and encouraged by campus-wide expectations for improvement; it leads to public discussions and is tangibly supported by the administration through resources and rewards.

So assessment is both old and new. It attaches new meanings to old vocabulary and new purposes to familiar techniques. While building on the academy's traditions, assessment fundamentally challenges habitual ways of doing business and conventional academic values. ■

CHAPTER 5

The Public Interest in Liberal Learning

A s *TAKING RESPONSIBILITY FOR THE QUALITY OF THE BACCALAUREATE DEGREE* (AAC&U 2004b) proposes, and this guide affirms, the three primary purposes of assessment are

- to provide students feedback on their performance;
- to help faculty members take stock of the collective achievement of students and, in so doing, evaluate the success of the educational program;
- to account to external stakeholders for the public trust they place in educational institutions.

> "We especially need imagination in science. It is not all mathematics, nor all logic, but it is somewhat beauty and poetry."
>
> Maria Mitchell

By fulfilling the first two obligations—which are inherent elements of good teaching—educators can also meet the third. What the broad lay public and policy makers do not yet fully understand, however, is that normed scores or survey responses cannot adequately reflect the kind of learning recommended by *Greater Expectations* (AAC&U 2002) and supported by business leaders and accreditors—deep, complex, and transformative learning. Essays and research projects, portfolios and capstones, online discussions and behavioral observations do a much better job. While statistics may not adequately capture the most important aspects of college learning, collections of evidence can document them. A combination of qualitative and quantitative measures of student learning can potentially construct the most robust picture. As Albert Einstein said, "Not everything that can be counted counts and not everything that counts can be counted." What eludes counting, however, can often be described and documented.

While consensus is developing on the important outcomes of college study, external pressures for accountability continue. By and large these calls for accountability ignore the question of *what* higher education should be accountable for. Policy makers somehow seem to disregard the complexity of the education that college students need to prepare for careers, for citizenship, and for lifetimes of continuous learning in the constantly changing twenty-first century. Instead of looking to assessment of general education learning outcomes (the nub of college study) as measures of institutional success, they look to surrogates like graduation rates, even as students swirl among institutions during their undergraduate years.

However, change seems imminent, although its attainment will still demand proactive involvement of the higher education community. The growing consensus suggests de facto understanding of the important capacities gained from college study. The next step will be to bring the outcomes themselves—outcomes of an engaged and practical liberal education—along with their proper assessments to bear on the question of "accountability for what?" As AAC&U and the academy reflect on the most appropriate ways to provide that accountability, these consensus outcomes may hold the key to a solution. When the desired, sophisticated learning is properly assessed in ways that remain true to the special character of college-level study and also respond to valid external demands, accountability will finally be based on what really matters in college.

U.S. society has a strong and legitimate interest in higher education's quality. Educators have responsibilities to the society that supports them, as well as to their students. The academy must set the terms of the accountability debate to ensure that discussions of assessment take account of the complexity of the educational process. Assessment as both an art and as a science is higher education's most powerful tool for developing the language, the concepts, and the evidence to respond appropriately to public calls for learning effectiveness. ∎

Assessment Methods Close-Up

THIS LAST CHAPTER is designed to help campuses choose methods of gathering evidence that are both appropriate to their goals and outcomes (step 4 in the step-by-step assessment process) and will lead to the desired improvement of general learning. It contains descriptions of eight direct methods that can form part of a comprehensive plan for assessing general education. Concrete examples further explicate the methods, as do rubrics, when appropriate. Rubrics clarify expectations about a specific outcome, so they are constructed with that outcome in mind. They are used to rate its achievement as demonstrated by student work; thus they can be combined with a variety of methods for gathering such artifacts. For example, Dordt College developed the rubric cited on page 41 to assess social responsibility as part of a common assignment; it could, however, also evaluate social responsibility in other contexts such as a capstone experience or a live discussion (a "performance"). All the rubrics in the following pages examine general education outcomes; one also looks at discipline-specific capacities.

Each assessment method generates its own particular evidence and is best adapted to certain circumstances. A portfolio, for example, could be organized to reveal changes in learning over time, whereas a single assignment embedded in a course would not. Some methods more easily lend themselves to the aggregation of data at the program or institutional level. This chapter provides guidance in evaluating each method's strengths and limitations. A campus's important questions about complex learning will ultimately determine the choice of approaches.

Many of the methods included require broad faculty conversations and collective work; they depend on collaboration across courses and among academic departments; and they rely on clear criteria and a shared understanding of what characterizes high-quality achievement. To harvest from assessment the maximum amount of rich, usable information about general education outcomes, the administration needs to provide the time and resources for ongoing faculty development. Investment of this sort will help build a campus-wide culture of evidence that both supports and is reinforced by assessment.

Portfolios

Portfolios originated with artists and graphic designers, who use them to display successful work. In the academy, portfolios first became popular in writing programs but are now quite common. Students collect examples of their work, select items to illustrate specific kinds of learning, write a reflective essay on the learning process, and connect their insights to past or future experiences. Through the steps of *collection*, *selection*, *reflection*, and *connection* portfolios can both demonstrate and deepen learning.

Campuses have now recognized the effectiveness of portfolios—hard copy and electronic—both as records of student work and as assessment tools. As records, they can illustrate development of knowledge and intellectual skills over time (longitudinally). As assessment tools, portfolios can provide evidence for interpretation at multiple levels: at the student level of self-assessment, where an individual reflects on his or her individual work; at the course level, where a professor (or a committee) reviews the range of work produced by the class; at the program level, where the faculty collectively examines students' achievement of general education goals; and even at the institutional level, where a campus documents the best work of graduates or the educational value added since freshman year. Portfolios can also be shared with external experts and stakeholders.

Virtually all direct and indirect assessment methods can provide evidence to fill a portfolio. However, to become a true assessment tool, portfolios need to be examined systematically using clearly defined criteria and collectively determined rating scales; institutions should also have a plan for using the information obtained to improve learning.

ADVANTAGES
Portfolios

- are adaptable to different levels, purposes (e.g., to show a cross-sectional snapshot or developmental change over time), and kinds of materials (e.g., written essays, taped performances, self-assessments);
- can elicit higher-order thinking through self-reflection;
- can document both the process and the product of learning;
- draw on the authentic work products of a student's education and can use them to provide external validation;
- actively engage students in the learning process.

POTENTIAL PROBLEMS AND THEIR SOLUTIONS
Portfolios

- can be labor-intensive to review, so use a sampling method for assessment and focus on a specific set of goals;
- can involve a complex gathering and reflection process that is difficult to oversee, so make students the responsible agents;
- can be cumbersome to store in paper form, so consider electronic portfolios;

A CAMPUS EXAMPLE

At **Indiana University–Purdue University Indianapolis** students build electronic portfolios to provide evidence that they have mastered the general education goals (called Principles of Undergraduate Learning). Included in the portfolios are carefully chosen pieces of work at introductory, intermediate, and advanced levels of each principle, as well as evidence of experiential learning. The matrix of evidence thereby created documents individual student progress over time. The goals of the electronic portfolio project include assessing learning of the principles from the course through institutional levels and engaging students with the concepts of the principles throughout the degree programs. Further information may be found at www.eport.iu.edu.

■ require trained reviewers, clear criteria, and consistent rating scales, so invest in faculty development.

RUBRICS USED IN PORTFOLIO ASSESSMENT

Source: **Portland State University**. For more information, see www.pdx.edu/advising/ unst_goals.html.

Nature of the rubrics: A total of four independent rubrics, one for each general education goal, are used by groups of faculty members to assess student portfolios for evidence of learning. The four have been condensed below into a single chart (a quantitative literacy rubric, which is a subsection of the communication goal, was omitted for brevity). The portfolios primarily serve program-level assessment.

Scores: Holistic scores range from one to six, with each described by multiple performance criteria. Only three of the six levels are shown below.

Possible adaptations (all of which are actually in use at Portland State):

■ Use for formative and/or summative assessment with individual student assignments.

■ Use for self-evaluation by students or formatively by peers and teachers at any time in the learning process.

■ Develop somewhat more analytical rubrics by scoring student work for each important criterion.

University Studies goals	Level 2: Does most or many of the following	Level 4: Does most of the following	Level 6: Consistently does all or almost all of the following
Inquiry and critical thinking	■ misinterprets evidence ■ draws unwarranted conclusions ■ seldom explains reasons	■ demonstrates basic ability to analyze, interpret ■ occasionally questions sources	■ accurately interprets evidence, etc. ■ identifies salient arguments ■ thoughtfully analyzes and evaluates
Communication: writing	■ makes serious errors in sentence structure, usage, mechanics ■ displays little development of ideas, so difficult to follow ■ fails to communicate effectively	■ makes some errors in sentence structure, mechanics ■ usually supports generalizations ■ displays some lack of focus but no serious organizational weaknesses	■ thinks lucidly and complexly ■ demonstrates clear and varied communication ■ evidences control of diction, syntactic variety, and usage
Diversity of human experience	■ fails to locate self in broader context of human experiences ■ shows only a basic comprehension of some issues in diversity	■ demonstrates a working knowledge of diverse peoples and societies ■ analyzes some issues, understands some situations through concepts and theory	■ views issues from multiple perspectives ■ comprehensively understands diversity issues
Ethics and social responsibility	■ mentions some issues, does not discuss meaningfully ■ reveals some evidence of self-reflection about ethical issues but is superficial	■ thoughtfully analyzes situations of ethical and social responsibility ■ contemplates impact of personal ethical choices	■ shows deep awareness of how ethical issues and social responsibility influence personal choices ■ constructs independent meaning and interpretations

Capstone experiences

A capstone experience, as the culmination of a program of study, can take many forms: a traditional scholarly paper, laboratory or field research, an individual or group project, a practicum. When designed to truly "cap" prior learning, the experience does not so much teach new material as allow students to review, make connections, and apply their knowledge to new problems or in new environments. Capstones are usually located in the major, but some institutions require them in general education (e.g., Portland State University) or design them to promote integration of general learning with more specialized knowledge. The value of the capstone experience can be heightened if the public is invited to witness students' work (e.g., through external evaluator review or presentation in a poster session open to the campus).

For assessment purposes, a program's faculty can collectively survey the work produced (or samples thereof), looking for evidence of the complex, integrated learning expected of all graduates. Taken as a whole, the year's "vintage" provides information about the program's strengths and weaknesses. A post-graduation retreat provides an ideal opportunity for the faculty to discuss findings and plan changes in curriculum, pedagogy, or other programmatic elements. If the capstone is used as a bookend together with a first-year experience, it can provide a longitudinal look at value-added learning over time.

ADVANTAGES
Capstone experiences

- can demonstrate cumulative learning, integration, and transferable intellectual skills;
- easily combine assessment of general and disciplinary learning;
- motivate students because they are directly linked to courses of study and often to future professions;
- provide an occasion for department-level collaborative discussion and interpretation;
- invite external comment and can serve to provide external validation.

POTENTIAL PROBLEMS AND THEIR SOLUTIONS
Capstone experiences

- may present difficulties in reaching all students of a cohort during their final semester, so plan fall and spring options and require capstones for graduation;
- may require an additional course, but this can be avoided by incorporating capstones into an existing senior requirement;
- may not take into account disciplinary differences, so allow multiple variations on a theme, possibly with a common set of principles;
- may require clarification of criteria as well as issues of confidentiality and aggregation to distinguish between the capstone's roles as a culmination of individual student work and as a vehicle for program assessment.

A CAMPUS EXAMPLE

Students at **Southern Illinois University Edwardsville** complete a senior assignment in the major meant to cap disciplinary as well as general education learning. Designed by department faculty to "make visible" the learning required for the degree—whether it occurs in the major program or in general education—the assignments are generally assessed using rubrics aligned with the desired outcomes that probe for several different kinds of evidence. Individual students receive feedback on their accomplishments while the data also serve at the program level to shape curricular and pedagogical improvements. The process of collectively designing and scoring senior assignments has improved the culture of faculty collaboration. For more information, see www.siue.edu/assessment.

Source: The economics department at **California State University, Sacramento**. For more information, see www.csus.edu/acaf/Assessment/econasmt.htm.

Nature of the rubric: Both discipline-specific and general learning is assessed summatively in an assignment for senior economics majors. Three faculty members independently score the capstone project and their ratings are averaged.

Scores: The total score from each reader (which can range from five to fifteen points) results from assessment in five outcome areas, each worth a maximum of three points.

Possible adaptations:

- Use the rubric in self-assessments and peer and faculty assessments during the formative stages of the capstone project.

- Develop each of the five areas into an independent assessment to follow students' capabilities on the way to senior-level competence.

Assessment goals/ objectives	Score definition	Total points
Understand and apply economic concepts and theories	3. understands and applies economic concepts and theories in a clear and effective manner 2. describes economic concepts, but does not clearly understand or apply them 1. does not understand or apply economic concepts; is confused	
Think critically and solve problems	3. identifies question at hand, thinks critically and solves problems in an illuminating way 2. identifies question at hand, but fails to think critically and solve problems 1. does not identify questions at hand, and fails to think critically and solve problems	
Use mathematics and statistics to facilitate the understanding of economic data	3. cites and uses mathematics or statistics, and brings them to bear on the issue/topic at hand 2. cites and uses mathematics or statistics that are of limited value or cites but does not use 1. does not cite or use sufficient (or any) mathematics or statistics regarding the topic/issue	
Use computers and other technologies to access, retrieve, and analyze data	3. cites an appropriate data source, presents and engages the information, examines and assesses it 2. cites an appropriate primary data source, but merely repeats the information, does not analyze it 1. does not identify a primary data source, or cites an inappropriate source	
Communicate findings both orally and in writing	3. clearly communicates findings orally and stimulates interest and discussion from the audience; communicates findings in writing in a clear and stimulating manner 2. communicates findings orally, but fails to stimulate interest from the audience and/or communicates findings in writing in an unclear manner 1. fails to orally communicate findings in a meaningful way and/or fails to communicate findings in writing	

Performances

Performances are simply the things students do that one can observe in action—a virtually limitless array of activities, from carrying out a lab experiment or singing an aria to teaching a class, taking a medical history, giving a speech, or mediating a disagreement. Unlike a piece of student work (an essay, a blueprint, or a painting, for example), the performance is ephemeral unless captured on tape or disk. Even when so recorded for repeated viewing, performances can be difficult to assess, so the development of usable rubrics and adequate training for raters are both of particular importance.

Because performances may be the only way to assess certain kinds of learning, it is essential to include them in the repertoire of assessment options. In addition, performances move both the student and the instructor from talk about a discipline or field to its actual practice, thereby adding an important dimension to traditional classroom practice. While posing challenges to instructors and students alike, performances also promise great benefits.

ADVANTAGES

Performances

- have strong face validity;
- emphasize what the student can do, thus are integrative, active, motivating, and reflective of real-world situations;
- provide a non-written way to demonstrate achievement, thereby giving students the message that doing is as important as knowing;
- promote self-assessment, internalization of standards, and a coaching relationship between students and faculty (especially when presented to external reviewers);
- are highly adaptable, even to liberal arts disciplines.

POTENTIAL PROBLEMS AND THEIR SOLUTIONS

Performances

- can be labor-intensive, time-consuming, and expensive to organize, so review a sample of student performances;
- require clear definitions of criteria and rating scales and careful training of reviewers, so regard the process as an educational investment;
- may frighten off insecure students, so embed in routine, nonthreatening situations (e.g., internships, clinical settings) and remind students they must eventually demonstrate employability.

A RUBRIC USED TO ASSESS THE PERFORMANCE OF PUBLIC SPEAKING

Source: **University of Alaska Southeast**. Effective oral communication—including interviewing, leading discussions, and public speaking—is an expectation of baccalaureate graduates. Students take a required course and also practice speaking across the curriculum. For more information, see www.uas.alaska.edu/humanities/programs/portfolio/comm-assess-fac-guide.htm.

A CAMPUS EXAMPLE

Many different procedures exist for assessing student teachers as they "perform" in a classroom, most requiring an observer to watch and then rate the quality of selected teaching behaviors; any number of these behaviors demonstrate learning outcomes of general education. The **University of Delaware** uses both a "Formative Student Teacher Observation Form" and a "Final Student Teacher Evaluation" with identical elements for observation and assessment of each. Targeted general education outcomes include communication integration, understanding of diversity, problem solving, critical thinking, and collaborative strategies. These skills, visible in the student teacher's work, also become learning objectives in the lessons they design. For more details, see www.udel.edu/dcte/ocs/superhandbook/wordfiles/657FormativeObs.doc.

Nature of the rubric: Observers are provided criteria (performance standards) for the three levels (unsatisfactory, satisfactory, and excellent) of eight specific competencies relevant to speech preparation and delivery. Examples of some criteria are inserted into cells of the following chart as illustrations.

Scores: Observers write comments in each of eight competency categories and provide a holistic rating using the three levels.

Possible adaptation: Use as self- and peer-assessment form during delivery of speeches.

Eight public speaking competencies	Speaking performance ratings			Comments
	Unsatisfactory	Satisfactory	Excellent	
1. Chooses and narrows a topic appropriately for the audience and occasion	[topic inconsistent with purpose, cannot be adequately treated in time limitation, no evidence of audience analysis]	[topic choice generally consistent with purpose, reasonable for time constraints, appropriate audience analysis]	[topic clearly consistent with purposes, totally amenable to time limitations; unusually insightful audience analysis]	
2. Communicates the thesis/specific purpose in a manner appropriate for audience and occasion				
3. Provides appropriate supporting material based on the audience and occasion	[vaguely related, detracts from speech]	[logically related, adds a measurable level of interest]	[unarguably linked, decidedly enhances]	
4. Uses an organizational pattern appropriate to topic, audience, occasion, and purpose				
5. Uses language that is appropriate to the audience, occasion, and purpose and demonstrates an ability to insert spontaneous comments in adapting ideas to the specific audience				
6. Uses vocal variety in rate, pitch, and intensity to heighten and maintain interest. Uses pronunciation, grammar, and articulation appropriate to designated audience				
7. Uses physical behaviors that support the verbal message and communicates engagement with audience through confidence, sincerity, and enthusiasm for the topic	[posture, gestures, eye contact, etc. fail to engage audience]	[acceptable posture, etc. shows some enthusiasm]	[posture, etc. actively engages audience]	
8. Uses visual aids appropriate to audience, occasion, and purpose				

Common assignments, secondary readings, and other embedded assessments

To embed an assessment means to make it part of the regular business of a course, requiring nothing more than students' completion of the assignments in the syllabus. Embedding assessment is an efficient way to collect high-quality, direct evidence of learning with minimal disruption and maximum utility.

One embedding technique is to give a piece of student work a "secondary reading" in addition to the primary reading it receives by the professor to assign a grade. For example, an assessment committee could sample a set of research papers from a class in American history, asking general education questions about historical perspective, critical thinking, writing, or information literacy skills. The history department could do something similar to answer questions about deep historical knowledge of majors. Such secondary readings enable student work to do double duty: it can be used both to evaluate an individual's achievement and to assess a course or a program.

Another way to embed assessment is by asking students in a number of different courses to complete a common assignment. For example, students in a range of introductory anthropology and sociology courses might be asked to respond to a common reading using guiding questions that reflect the faculty's definition of higher-order thinking in the social sciences. A less cumbersome variation would have examinations include just one common question. If the common assignment is administered across a wide range of disciplines, a template allows instructors to customize content to their courses while the guiding questions or the structure of the essay conform to the collectively designed template.

ADVANTAGES

Embedded assessments

- use work that students already complete for a course, thereby ensuring typical quality of effort;
- are efficient and economical, with potentially rich results;
- are flexible, can be adapted to all fields, and respect disciplinary differences;
- have face validity;
- respect local autonomy while encouraging collaboration.

POTENTIAL PROBLEMS AND THEIR SOLUTIONS

Embedded assessments

- can require considerable coordination and political negotiation when done through common assignments, so keep the task simple (e.g., use a few questions if an entire common assignment is impractical);
- can be labor-intensive to score, so focus on the most important questions that need to be answered;
- require careful definition of rubrics and training of reviewers, so make the investment in faculty development.

A CAMPUS EXAMPLE

In academic year 2002–3, **Capital Community College** used a common assignment to assess quantitative reasoning, one of the institution's general education goals. Instructors in different disciplines—ranging from ESL to marketing to biology—embedded the assignment into their course syllabi. In the fall semester, student read a newspaper article on changes in income distribution throughout Connecticut and then answered a series of increasingly complex mathematical questions using an accompanying data table. Students also were asked to score the degree of difficulty of the questions and write an explanation of how the data clarified the larger discussion of poverty. Individual professors tailored the instructions for the essay to fit the topic of their courses. Students were graded for their individual work in ways appropriate to the course. When scored for assessment purposes, a sampling of the five hundred completed assignments indicated the general level of students' mathematics skills. Data interpretation, including comparison to math courses completed, led to a series of recommendations for improvement.

A RUBRIC USED TO ASSESS QUANTITATIVE REASONING AS PART OF
AN EMBEDDED COMMON ASSIGNMENT

Source: **Capital Community College** (see sidebar description of the common assignment that, together with the rubric, was developed by Professors Kathleen Herron, Lynn
Marino, and Peter Wursthorn). For more information, visit www.ccc.commnet.edu/slat.

Nature of the rubric: Developed by the mathematics professors on the assessment team,
the rubric examines four areas of mathematical abilities to get a measure of quantitative
reasoning competence.

Scores: A holistic score for the entire common assignment is obtained by averaging the
analytic scores for each of the four ability areas (using a scale of one to four points).

Possible adaptations:

- Develop scoring standards for each level in each ability area to tighten
  interpretations.
- Use as a model for developing rubrics in other disciplines that can be
  either holistic or analytical.

Numbers/operations	Algebra/geometry	Graphing	Mathematical modeling
Use arithmetic operations to: ■ arrange numbers in order ■ find maxima and minima ■ find medians ■ find percentages	Use variables and solve equations, both linear and exponential, to answer questions about real-world data	■ interpret and convey numerical information in appropriate graphs ■ graph a linear equation ■ interpret slope	Connect mathematics concepts and methods to real-world situations
4	*Superior*: (85-100% correct) Nearly flawless.		
3	*Proficient*: (70-85% correct) Equations are nearly correct. Models will be reasonable and meaningful. There is much better use of equations than for "essential." For the most part, graphs will be correct.		
2	*Essential*: (30-70% correct) There is evidence of comprehension and a reasoned approach to the problem. There will be errors, and logic may be hard to discern. Estimates will be better than for those "in progress." There may be an attempt to use an equation.		
1	*In progress*: (0-30% correct) Floundering, very little idea of what is to be done.		

Classroom assessment techniques/action research

Classroom assessment techniques (CATs) were developed by Thomas Angelo and K. Patricia Cross in the mid-1980s as part of the emerging assessment movement. Conceived as an alternative to macro-level state mandates and standardized testing, CATs locate assessment of student learning right in the classroom and put its control into the hands of individual instructors. In a series of publications, Angelo and Cross provided dozens of activities that a teacher can employ to gather both direct and indirect evidence of student learning and make mid-course corrections. Similarly, electronic "clickers" (which immediately register and tabulate student responses) are an increasingly popular way to gather just-in-time input on the day's studies.

Although the CATs were originally intended for formative assessment at the course level, they can be adapted to the program level and also help answer summative questions. For example, instructors across a range of courses can agree to administer one particular CAT at a selected point in the semester, pool their findings, and then review the results program-wide. Classroom assessment is sometimes called "action research" when an instructor or program collects findings over time, identifies patterns, uses the data to improve learning, and shares the results publicly. Recent interest in the scholarship of teaching and learning has created a growing community of practitioners involved in such research.

ADVANTAGES

Classroom assessment techniques

- have maximum relevance and usefulness for immediate improvement because assessment takes place at the point of student learning;
- can be conducted continuously to emphasize that teaching is a formative, evolving process;
- can provide feedback on what students know and can do, how they got there, and what helps or hinders learning;
- engage students in their learning, motivate them to monitor themselves, and help them become reflective learners;
- communicate that professors care about students, but also respect faculty autonomy.

POSSIBLE PROBLEMS AND THEIR SOLUTIONS

Classroom assessment techniques

- are highly dependent on the cooperation of individuals, so create a culture that values and supports the entire assessment process;
- can present challenges in generalizing to program or institution level, so encourage an ongoing forum for sharing approaches and results.

EXAMPLES OF CLASSROOM ASSESSMENT TECHNIQUES

Instructors at many institutions use a wide variety of classroom assessment techniques and are often supported in their efforts by centers of effective teaching. At **Indiana University**, the Office of Campus Instructional Consulting has prepared materials to help faculty members understand the advantages of classroom assessment techniques; the following chart (largely drawn from Angelo and Cross 1993), in an expanded form, is available online at www.iub.edu/-teaching/feedback.shtml.

Technique	Description	What to do with the data	Effort required
Minute paper	During the last few minutes of the class period, ask students to answer on a half-sheet of paper: "What is the most important point you learned today?" and "What point remains least clear to you?" The purpose is to elicit data about students' comprehension of a particular class session.	Review responses and note any useful comments. During the following class periods emphasize the issues raised by your students' comments.	Preparation: Low In class: Low Analysis: Low
Memory matrix	Students fill in cells of a two-dimensional diagram for which the instructor has provided labels. For example, in a music course, labels might consist of periods (Baroque, Classical) by countries (Germany, France, Britain); students enter composers in cells to demonstrate their ability to remember and classify key concepts.	Tally the numbers of correct and incorrect responses in each cell. Analyze differences both between and among the cells. Look for patterns among the incorrect responses and decide what might be the cause(s).	Preparation: Medium In class: Medium Analysis: Medium
Directed paraphrasing	Ask students to write a layman's "translation" of something they have just learned—geared to a specified individual or audience—to assess their ability to comprehend and transfer concepts.	Categorize student responses according to characteristics you feel are important. Analyze the responses both within and across categories, noting ways you could address student needs.	Preparation: Low In class: Medium Analysis: Medium
One-sentence summary	Students summarize knowledge of a topic by constructing a single sentence that answers the questions "Who does what to whom, when, where, how, and why?" The purpose is to require students to select only the defining features of an idea.	Evaluate the quality of each summary quickly and holistically. Note whether students have identified the essential concepts of the class topic and their interrelationships. Share your observations with your students.	Preparation: Low In class: Medium Analysis: Medium
Application cards	After teaching about an important theory, principle, or procedure, ask students to write down at least one real-world application for what they have just learned to determine how well they can transfer their learning.	Quickly read once through the applications and categorize them according to their quality. Pick out a broad range of examples and present them to the class.	Preparation: Low In class: Low Analysis: Medium
Student-generated test questions	Allow students to write test questions and model answers for specified topics in a format consistent with course exams. This will give students the opportunity to evaluate the course topics, reflect on what they understand, and what might be good test items.	Make a rough tally of the questions your students propose and the topics that they cover. Evaluate the questions and use the good ones as prompts for discussion. You may also want to revise the questions and use them on the upcoming exam.	Preparation: Medium In class: High Analysis: High May be part of homework

RUBRICS

Classroom assessment techniques do not generally use rubrics since the student responses provide immediate feedback about the progress of the class. The method, however, can appropriately be used both in general education and in disciplinary classes (to elicit information about general learning content, intellectual skills, or dispositions as well as about more specialized knowledge).

Local tests

In contrast to a test marketed by a company and designed for application nationwide, a local test is developed by a campus for use with its own students. The testing instrument can be tailored to the intellectual content, curricular design, teaching practices, and expectations of the campus's educational programs. It can lend itself to rapid adaptation if those conditions change. Local tests need not conform to the familiar multiple-choice format; they can be essay-based, offer a mix of closed- and open-ended responses, or incorporate other features such as the "gripe sheet," which allows students to take issue with particular questions. By including a gripe sheet, faculty members can balance the efficiencies of short-answer testing with the richer information gathered when students demonstrate deeper thinking.

Local tests can be time-consuming and require broad faculty participation for development, administration, and interpretation of results. However, the process can also promote faculty ownership of learning by solidifying collective commitment to outcomes, curricular elements, and assessment methods. Local tests do not allow comparison of one institution against another. However, repeated testing does make possible a record of improvement, stagnation, or regression over time.

ADVANTAGES

Local tests

- have content validity because they are designed for local learning conditions;
- can reflect the campus's culture and teaching-learning processes;
- can be integrative and highly creative in format;
- elicit high-quality student effort if course-embedded;
- provide directly relevant and useful information.

POTENTIAL PROBLEMS AND THEIR SOLUTIONS

Local tests

- may focus on surface learning, so provide a gripe sheet to extract deeper reflection;
- may lack norms for reference, so supplement with a commercial test if norms are essential;
- may contain ambiguous items or offer questionable reliability and validity, so pilot the test to identify and evaluate such problems prior to any large-scale administration;
- can be seen as threatening, so keep the focus on useful information for learning improvement, not on test scores per se.

A CAMPUS EXAMPLE

California Polytechnic State University uses a locally developed proficiency exam as an option for students to demonstrate competence in written communication prior to graduation. Administered after students have completed ninety credits, the two-hour essay exam is designed to assess written communication, analysis, and critical thinking. After students read a short passage, a prompt asks them to summarize the writer's points and then argue for their own position on the topic. An essay of at least five hundred words is expected to demonstrate summarizing, describing, defining, comparing/contrasting, analyzing, and arguing. Assessment looks at comprehension, organization, development, and expression; a well-defined rubric facilitates reliable scoring. The university's Web site contains student-friendly information on the assessment process, examples of reading passages and prompts, and samples of scored student essays. A campus writing center helps students prepare for the exam. See www.calpoly.edu/~wrtskils/writla wpe.htm.

A RUBRIC USED TO ASSESS SOCIAL RESPONSIBILITY AS PART OF A
LOCALLY DEVELOPED TEST

Source: **Dordt College.** For more information, see www.dordt.edu/publications/
assessment/apdxb.shtml.

Nature of the rubric: The rubric is used to assess, both as part of freshman orientation and
toward the end of a student's career, a required essay on social challenges. Raters receive
elaborated criteria for all the ability areas and also stimulus questions to help calibrate
their scoring. The following table has been excerpted from a more comprehensive rubric.

Scores: Provides a holistic score for the entire essay and analytic scores (on a seven-point
scale) for each ability area.

Possible adaptations: Use in formative, summative, and self-assessments between first and
last years to track progress and foster growth of the capacities.

Scoring criteria	1 2	3 4 5	6 7
Forms of moral judgment	■ external authorities, arbitrary view of right and wrong ■ doing what you're told	■ internalized authorities, knows answers but not sure why ■ right and wrong depend on/ relative to situation	■ attempts to understand and articulate norms and principles derived from internalized understanding of the value implications of one's faith commitment
Worldview	■ simplistic ■ not aware of having a worldview as explicit and interrelated system of beliefs, assumptions, and commitments	■ worldview consists primarily of a synthesis of conventional beliefs, assumptions, and morals ■ little evidence of reflection on the more generalized implications of assumptions, beliefs, or commitments	■ awareness of one's worldview as explicit system based on a deliberate, conscious affirmation of values, assumptions, beliefs, and commitments ■ can evaluate others' systems from this vantage point
Acceptance of personal responsibility in response to challenges	■ not my problem ■ shows little empathy ■ situation judged in terms of own needs and concerns ■ simplistic solutions without evidence of personal commitment to action	■ aware of personal impact and need for involvement ■ unclear as to the nature and extent of communal responsibility and action ■ solutions/suggestions are broader in scope, but not comprehensive	■ clearly sees self as involved and responsible for dealing with issues in concrete, clearly articulated ways ■ sensitive to the broader communal impact of individual action
Historical/structural basis	■ no mention or acknowledgment of historical development or impact of societal structures ■ problems based exclusively on personal responsibility	■ mentions historical development and/or societal structures, but focus is on personal, immediate, or situational influences	■ explicitly states that problems often have a historical context, and that societal or cultural structures contribute to individual and societal problems

Commercial tests

Commercial tests can be purchased from such organizations as Educational Testing Service and American College Testing. Mostly these instruments use multiple-choice format, although writing components have been incorporated recently. The terms "standardized" and "objective" are often applied to commercially available tests, implying that other assessment methods meet neither criterion. But this distinction is not entirely accurate. Standardized refers to uniform test conditions and scoring procedures, so ratings from multiple administrations are presumed to be reliable (i.e., have the same value). However, locally developed tests and other assessments can also maintain consistency.

Short-answer tests may or may not be objective (cultural biases certainly exist), but alternative methods are not necessarily subjective. Expert judgments and scoring based on rubrics, for example, constrained by empirical findings and agreed-upon standards, are far from arbitrary, while training can enhance inter-rater reliability. Commercial test scores are usually normed (i.e., reported as a percentile of all test takers) rather than being criterion-referenced (compared to specific criteria of achievement). While normed scores allow an institution to compare itself to other institutions, they do not distinguish between areas of successful or poor performance; thus their utility for improving educational practices is generally limited.

ADVANTAGES

Commercial tests

- are a traditional, widely recognized, and accepted means of assessment;
- require little on-campus time or labor;
- prepare students for licensure and other certifications;
- offer longitudinal data;
- are technically high quality.

POSSIBLE PROBLEMS AND THEIR SOLUTIONS

Commercial tests

- provide poor validity if not closely aligned to assessment questions or students' actual learning, so use with caution;
- reinforce a limited view of learning as factual recall and of assessment as simple testing if in short-answer format;
- provide little insight into the level of understanding or quality of thinking behind the answer, so supplement with other methods;
- give students no opportunity to construct their own answers or demonstrate important affective traits (e.g., persistence, creativity) if in short-answer format.

A RUBRIC USED TO ASSESS WRITING AS PART OF A COMMERCIAL TEST

*Source: **How the Essay is Scored**.* Copyright © 2005 by the **College Board**. Reprinted with permission. All rights reserved. www.collegeboard.com. See www.collegeboard.com/student/testing/sat/about/sat/essay_scoring.html.

AN ALTERNATIVE TO COMMERCIAL TESTS

The **Collegiate Learning Assessment** (CLA), which is being developed for the Rand Corporation's Council for Aid to Education, provides both cross-sectional and longitudinal assessment of general education's higher-order intellectual skills. CLA uses performance-based instruments to examine the value added by colleges in important areas of learning (critical thinking, analytic reasoning, and written communication). The cross-sectional assessment compares freshman and seniors, while the longitudinal assessment tests a student cohort in its first, second, and last years. CLA combines two types of instruments as it asks students to draw on data, pictures and/or texts to reach conclusions and integrate knowledge: a "real-life" task (e.g., preparing a policy recommendation) and writing prompts to solicit complex ideas supported by examples. Individual student results are externally scored and then aggregated to better understand each college and university's unique contributions to learning. CLA's design attempts to avoid the potential problems of commercially available tests. For more information, see www.cae.org/content/pro_collegiate.htm.

Nature of the rubric: A holistic scoring of the new SAT essay that approximates the level of entering freshman writing. Two trained raters score each essay based on a rubric that was formatted into the following chart.

Scores: Provides a holistic score on a scale of one to six.

Possible adaptation: Use as the basis for an analytic rubric to help develop writing, especially at the first-year college level.

Score	An essay in this category is...	A typical essay...
6	outstanding, demonstrating clear and consistent mastery, although it may have a few minor errors	■ effectively and insightfully develops a point of view on the issue and demonstrates outstanding critical thinking, using clearly appropriate examples, reasons, and other evidence to support its position ■ is well organized and clearly focused, demonstrating clear coherence and smooth progression of ideas ■ exhibits skillful use of language, using a varied, accurate, and apt vocabulary ■ demonstrates meaningful variety in sentence structure ■ is free of most errors in grammar, usage, and mechanics
5	effective, demonstrating reasonably consistent mastery, although it will have occasional errors or lapses in quality	■ effectively develops a point of view on the issue and demonstrates strong critical thinking, generally using appropriate examples, reasons, and other evidence to support its position ■ is well organized and focused, demonstrating coherence and progression of ideas ■ exhibits facility in the use of language, using appropriate vocabulary ■ demonstrates variety in sentence structure ■ is generally free of most errors in grammar, usage, and mechanics
4	competent, demonstrating adequate mastery, although it will have lapses in quality	■ develops a point of view on the issue and demonstrates competent critical thinking, using adequate examples, reasons, and other evidence to support its position ■ is generally organized and focused, demonstrating some coherence and progression of ideas ■ exhibits adequate but inconsistent facility in the use of language, using generally appropriate vocabulary ■ demonstrates some variety in sentence structure ■ has some errors in grammar, usage, and mechanics
3	inadequate, but demonstrates developing mastery, and is marked by one or more of the following weaknesses	■ develops a point of view on the issue, demonstrating some critical thinking but may do so inconsistently or use inadequate examples, reasons, or other evidence to support its position ■ is limited in its organization or focus, but may demonstrate some lapses in coherence or progression of ideas ■ displays developing facility in the use of language, but sometimes uses weak vocabulary or inappropriate word choice ■ lacks variety or demonstrates problems in sentence structure ■ contains an accumulation of errors in grammar, usage, and mechanics
2	seriously limited, demonstrating little mastery, and is flawed by one or more of the following weaknesses	■ develops a point of view on the issue that is vague or seriously limited, demonstrating weak critical thinking, providing inappropriate or insufficient examples, reasons, or other evidence to support its position ■ is poorly organized and/or focused, or demonstrates serious problems with coherence or progression of ideas ■ displays very little facility in the use of language, using very limited vocabulary or incorrect word choice ■ demonstrates frequent problems in sentence structure ■ contains errors in grammar, usage, and mechanics so serious that meaning is somewhat obscured
1	fundamentally lacking, demonstrating very little or no mastery, and is severely flawed by one or more of the following weaknesses	■ develops no viable point of view on the issue, or provides little or no evidence to support its position ■ is disorganized or unfocused, resulting in a disjointed or incoherent essay ■ displays fundamental errors in vocabulary ■ demonstrates severe flaws in sentence structure ■ contains pervasive errors in grammar, usage, or mechanics that persistently interfere with meaning
0	not written on the essay assignment	

Course-management programs

Increasingly, electronic course-management programs (like Blackboard and WebCT) have made it possible for professors and students to interact in new ways; sharing lecture notes and supplementary readings, communicating via e-mail, and participating in threaded conversations outside of class all extend the classroom beyond its traditional boundaries. The programs also allow students to create electronic portfolios of their work and blogs expressing their personal views. Programs associated with textbooks can include testing and surveying options.

The potential of course-management programs as assessment tools has barely been realized. Most interesting, perhaps, is the capability to keep a running record of discussions that would be lost if they took place in the classroom. If a course (or general education program) expects students to develop critical questioning, collaborative decision making, or an ethical perspective, for example, these capacities may be captured well—over time—in a threaded electronic discussion. A software program like NUD*IST can be used for efficient qualitative analysis of extended prose passages.

For the most part, however, commercial course-management programs have not been designed by educators familiar with contemporary approaches to assessment. Thus some of these programs' most highly touted assessment features (e.g., item banks and templates for multiple-choice tests, short-answer quizzes, and surveys) may not yet reflect best assessment practices.

AN OPEN-SOURCE COURSE-MANAGEMENT PROGRAM

If an institution is interested in free course-management software it might look at the **Sakai Project**, a recent cooperative venture of several major universities. Launched by the University of Michigan, Indiana University, MIT, Stanford, and other partners, Sakai is now being further developed and implemented on more than twenty campuses. With the software design occurring at different universities, it is to be hoped that the knowledge of assessment experts will help inform the technical work so Sakai can become a powerful assessment tool. For more information, visit the project's Web site at www.sakaiproject.org.

ADVANTAGES

Course-management programs

- are adaptable to a wide range of learning goals, disciplines, and environments;
- use work produced electronically as a normal part of the course;
- record ephemera that are normally impossible or cumbersome to capture;
- can preserve a large volume of material;
- are efficient, low-cost, and completely nonintrusive;
- allow prompt feedback and develop students' meta-cognition when assessment results are shared.

POTENTIAL PROBLEMS AND THEIR SOLUTIONS

Course-management programs

- rely heavily on student writing skill and comfort with technology, so incorporate into a comprehensive assessment approach;
- pose challenges to levels of aggregation beyond the individual course, so develop precise rubrics;
- can involve managing a large volume of material, so use built-in data management tools;
- may promote surface rather than deep learning, so use the incorporated tests and quizzes with caution and supplement with authentic tasks;
- may make direct observation of student performances difficult and encourage the collection of indirect evidence, so supplement the built-in survey tools with other methods. ■

Appendix — Practical Tools
ASSESSMENT, STEP-BY-STEP CHECKLIST

STEP 1: Understand the mission, values, traditions, and aspirations of your institution and the role of general education in advancing them.

QUESTIONS TO CONSIDER:

❑ What are our institution's values, intellectual traditions, or guiding principles that should be evident in the general education program?

❑ What distinguishes education at our institution?

❑ What makes our general education distinctive from that at comparable campuses?

❑ How are our intellectual traditions or values reflected in our approach to assessment? Is there congruence between educational ends and assessment means?

STEP 2: Define key learning goals for your students.

QUESTIONS TO CONSIDER:

❑ What does the faculty agree that all students graduating from our institution should know and be able to do?

❑ What skills, capacities, and knowledge will prepare our students—whatever their areas of concentration—for the complex, diverse, and globally interdependent world of the twenty-first century?

❑ Are these goals widely known and owned by the entire campus community? How can we enhance buy-in?

STEP 3: Turn your broad learning goals into assessable outcomes; specify the level of accomplishment desired.

QUESTIONS TO CONSIDER:

❑ Have our broad learning goals been subdivided into more specific outcomes and performance indicators?

❑ What exactly do we expect our students to know and be able to do with their knowledge in their freshman, sophomore, junior, and senior years?

❑ How much, and in what ways, do we want our students' level of achievement to increase from novice to advanced over their years of college study?

❑ What burning questions does our faculty most want to answer?

STEP 4: Select methods for gathering evidence of learning that are appropriate to your desired goals and outcomes.

QUESTIONS TO CONSIDER:

❏ What assessment method or methods would best provide direct evidence of learning to answer our questions?

❏ What are we already doing that can also serve assessment purposes?

❏ What methods would be in keeping with our mission and values?

STEP 5: Determine the crucial points at which you need to gather evidence.

QUESTIONS TO CONSIDER:

❏ What exactly are our expectations for students' development of knowledge, skills, and values over time?

❏ What are students already doing, in class or beyond, that can generate evidence for assessment purposes?

❏ Which are the most important data-collection points in our curriculum and for which outcomes?

❏ Are our plans effective yet manageable? How will we use the evidence gathered?

STEP 6: Close the improvement loop by ensuring that you interpret and use the evidence collected.

QUESTIONS TO CONSIDER:

❏ What are our plans for interpreting evidence? Who will be involved? How will we manage and support the process?

❏ Are we satisfied with the learning achieved? If not, what changes are needed?

❏ What resources are required and available to implement proposed changes?

❏ What obstacles to change exist and how can they be overcome?

❏ When will we revisit these changes to see whether they were successful?

❏ How will we communicate and celebrate our successes?

Ten Tips for Better Assessment, Summary

1. **Look for evidence of learning, not just statistics.**

2. **Remain focused first on improving the quality of student learning, then on assuring its quality.**

3. **Build on what is already occurring.**

4. **Make assessment ongoing, not episodic.**

5. **Divide the labor, share the responsibility.**

6. **Do not let the perfect be the enemy of the good.**

7. **Prioritize.**

8. **Experiment, take risks, be creative.**

9. **Tell the whole story.**

10. **Remember that assessment is both old and new.**

AN ASSESSMENT PLANNING MATRIX FOR GENERAL EDUCATION
LEARNING OUTCOMES ACROSS THE CURRICULUM IN THE SPIRIT OF *GREATER EXPECTATIONS*

Guiding questions for a campus:

- Which learning outcomes should be assessed at which critical points? How do they interrelate to form a comprehensive program that can demonstrate cumulative learning over time and across courses?
- What do we already have in place that could serve assessment purposes?
- What might we need to add?
- Which elements should be part of the general education program? Which demonstrate competency building in the major?

Note: A campus should substitute its own outcomes for the examples in the first and second columns.

Outcome area of the intentional learner	Learning outcomes	First-year general education experience (introductory or novice level)	Introduction to the major (introductory or novice level)	Intermediate courses in the major or general education (intermediate level)	Senior capstone or culminating experience in the major or general education (advanced/expert level)
Empowering intellectual and practical skills	■ written communication ■ oral communication ■ second-language proficiency ■ critical thinking ■ creative thinking ■ information literacy ■ quantitative literacy ■ intercultural skills and teamwork				
Informing knowledge from multiple disciplines	■ experience with various inquiry modes ■ knowledge of cultural artifacts ■ knowledge of the world and its problems ■ comfort with science and technology ■ experience with the arts ■ familiarity with the diversity of the U.S.				
The examined values of responsible life and citizenship	■ ethical perspectives ■ acceptance of difference ■ civic participation				
Integration	■ awareness of the learning process ■ ability to draw on different perspectives ■ ability to connect across disciplines ■ ability to apply theory to practice ■ ability to conduct research				

References

Anderson, Lorin W., David R. Krathwohl, Peter W. Airasian, Kathleen A. Cruikshank, Richard E. Mayer, Paul R. Pintrich, James Raths, and Merlin C. Wittrock. 2001. *A taxonomy for learning, teaching and assessing: A revision of Bloom's taxonomy of educational objectives.* New York: Addison Wesley Longman, Inc.

Angelo, Thomas A. 1995. Reassessing (and defining) assessment. *American Association for Higher Education Bulletin* 48 (3): 7.

Angelo, Thomas A., and K. Patricia Cross. 1993. *Classroom assessment techniques: A handbook for college teachers.* 2nd ed. San Francisco: Jossey-Bass.

Association of American Colleges and Universities. 2002. *Greater expectations: A new vision for learning as a nation goes to college.* Washington, DC: Association of American Colleges and Universities.

———. 2004a. *Our students' best work: A framework for accountability worthy of our mission.* Washington, DC: Association of American Colleges and Universities.

———. 2004b. *Taking responsibility for the quality of the baccalaureate degree.* Washington, DC: Association of American Colleges and Universities.

Astin, Alexander, Trudy W. Banta, K. Patricia Cross, Elaine El-Khawas, Peter T. Ewell, Pat Hutchings, Theodore J. Marchese, et al. 1992. *Principles of good practice for assessing student learning.* Washington, DC: American Association for Higher Education.

Barr, Robert B., and John Tagg. 1995. From teaching to learning: A new paradigm for undergraduate education. *Change* 27 (6): 12–25.

Bloom, Benjamin S., ed. 1956. *Taxonomy of educational objectives: The classification of educational goals.* New York: David McKay Company, Inc.

Dressel, Paul L., and Lewis B. Mayhew. 1954. *General education: Explorations in evaluation.* Washington, DC: American Council on Education.

Entwistle, Noel. 2001. Promoting deep learning through teaching and assessment. In *Assessment to promote deep learning: Insight from AAHE's 2000 and 1999 assessment conferences,* ed. Linda Suskie, 9–20. Washington, DC: American Association for Higher Education.

Leskes, Andrea. 2002. Beyond confusion: An assessment glossary. *Peer Review* 4 (2/3): 42–43.

Maki, Peggy. 2002. Developing an assessment plan to learn about student learning. American Association for Higher Education. www.aahe.org/assessment/assessmentplan.htm (accessed June 3, 2005).

Marra, Rose M. 2002. The ideal online learning environment for supporting epistemic development: Putting the puzzle together. *Quarterly Review of Distance Education* 3 (1): 15–31.

Palomba, Catherine A., and Trudy Banta. 1999. *Assessment essentials: Planning, implementing and improving assessment in higher education.* San Francisco: Jossey-Bass.

Perry, William G. 1970. *Forms of intellectual and ethical development in the college years: A scheme.* Repr., San Francisco: Jossey-Bass, 1999.

Ratcliff, James L., D. Kent Johnson, Steven M. La Nasa, and Jerry G. Gaff. 2001. *The status of general education in the year 2000: Summary of a national survey.* Washington, DC: Association of American Colleges and Universities.

Resnick, Lauren B. 1987. *Education and learning to think.* Washington, DC: National Academy Press.

Rogers, Gloria M. 2004. *Portfolios: The tool that rocks.* Presentation at the American Association for Higher Education assessment conference, Denver.

Tagg, John. 2003. *The learning paradigm college.* Bolton, MA: Anker Publishing Company Inc.

About the Authors

Andrea Leskes is vice president for education and quality initiatives at the Association of American Colleges and Universities (AAC&U). She joined the association in 1999 to lead the Greater Expectations initiative on the aims and best practices of undergraduate education for the twenty-first century. Leskes was the principal author of *Greater Expectations: A New Vision for Learning as a Nation Goes to College*. She also directs AAC&U's annual general education institute, writes regularly for the association's quarterly journals, and consults with campuses on curricular reform.

Leskes holds a PhD in cell biology from the Rockefeller University and a master's degree in French from the University of Massachusetts at Amherst. Her prior appointments include serving as vice president for academic affairs, dean of the university, and professor of comparative literature at the American University of Paris; vice provost for undergraduate education at Northeastern University; associate dean for humanities, arts, and social sciences at Brandeis University; and assistant dean of faculty at Dartmouth College. Dr. Leskes's publications span the fields of science, translation, and higher education.

Barbara D. Wright is an associate director at the Western Association of Schools and Colleges in Alameda, California. Prior to that appointment she served as assessment coordinator at Eastern Connecticut State University and as a professor of German at the University of Connecticut, Storrs. She is especially interested in qualitative approaches to the assessment of education's more elusive goals, and in the relationship of U.S. higher education to other social and political institutions.

From 1988 to 1990 Wright directed a project supported by the Fund for the Improvement of Postsecondary Education to assess general education at the University of Connecticut, and from 1990 to 1992 she directed the American Association for Higher Education's Assessment Forum. Dr. Wright served on the New England Association of Schools and Colleges' Commission on Institutions of Higher Education and on the advisory board of the New England Educational Assessment Network. Her publications reflect her appreciation for drama, whether of the Baroque or Brecht or the college classroom.

Wright holds a master's degree from Middlebury College and a PhD from the University of California, Berkeley, both in German. ■